TABLE OF CONTENTS

PREFACE: BUT I DON'T HAVE THE TIME

" The best thing about the future is that it comes one day at a time." - Abraham Lincoln

"But I don't have the time" is the phrase I often hear when I speak to people about turning their thoughts into actions. While we may fantasize about starting our own companies or developing our unique ideas, most of us don't have the financial liberty to quit our 9 to 5 jobs to work on our ideas full time. However, you can still successfully see your ideas come to fruition even while keeping your job. It just takes a little bit of extra effort.

Think about what you do when you come home from work. You have dinner with your family, play with the dog, take care of errands, and, for most of us, watch TV. According to a 2012 article from the *Daily News*, the average American spends more than thirty-four hours watching TV a week.[i] If you were being paid $150/hour that would translate to over $260,000 dollars per year.

Many of us don't even realize how we're spending our time. Before you dive into the rest of this book, I recommend keeping a diary of your activities for a few days to identify the amount of time each day that you could use to work on your ideas. You may be surprised at just how much free time you actually have.

Spending a few hours per week developing your idea instead of zoning out can quickly put you on the right track. Do you commute to work each day? An hour train ride is the perfect time to work on your concepts, outline thoughts, and create solid task lists. Make calls during your lunch break (use your personal cell phone, of course), and replace your usual Internet surfing with research and email follow-ups. With each small goal accomplished, your sense of accomplishment and motivation will grow, giving you the focus to move forward every chance you get.

This book will help you take that free time and develop your idea. By following the steps ahead, you can take your idea, get it made, and get it sold. It may or may not be a million dollar idea, but you'll see just how easy it is to take any good idea and have it produce an income. Maybe you'll get lucky and your idea will make you a billionaire, maybe you'll have to produce a few things to be able to say you can quit your job. In either case, 'appitalizing' on your idea will allow you to say you are an entrepreneur.

INTRODUCTION: WHY I AM TELLING MY STORY

"The difference between a successful person and other is not a lack of strength, not a lack of knowledge, but rather a lack of will." – Vince Lombardi, Pro-NFL coach

After speaking around the country about entrepreneurship and how I started my own companies, I've learned a lot of people have really phenomenal ideas that just need a little help getting the gears in motion. While I love seeing my own ideas take off, I'm even more excited by the prospect of helping develop a universal formula for success. Hence why I am writing this book. I want you to use it as a manual, a 101 course for entrepreneurship.

Beyond my own passion, I see the value that entrepreneurship has in our world. It pushes technology forward, challenging us as human beings to think and to evolve. I have met people with ideas that have real value for our society, but they are allowing minor roadblocks to get in their way and to prevent them from making an impact.

It is important to note that while my own experience is specifically with application development, the lessons in this book can be applied to all different products and services. Since speaking on the topic, I've had people come back to me to share their success stories - some developed apps, while one wrote a physics book! It's not the 'what' that matters; it's the 'how.'

In the United States, my parents' generation was told that after school, you get a job at a big corporation. Those big corporations, like GE, were the 'safe' jobs. You go in, do your job, keep your head down, and bring home a steady paycheck. But things have changed. After all the issues our country has faced economically no longer are there those safe jobs. Now is the time for entrepreneurs.

Outside the U.S., the same thing exists. There's nothing stopping someone in Japan, France, or South Africa from coming up with a good idea and bringing it to fruition. Creativity isn't limited to location, schooling or culture; anyone can come up with a great idea.

Being an entrepreneur isn't only about NOT having a boss. It's about following your passion. It's about taking what you love and making it a reality. Every time I see an e-mail or a tweet about one of my apps, it makes me smile from ear to ear. It blows my mind that someone out there pays me for what was an original idea in my head.

There's really nothing to stop you, except you. Have an idea? Great! Let's get it moving. Don't have an idea yet? Not to worry. There are ways of coming up with some. As you will read later, you can even ask people for ideas. Maybe there is someone you know who has an issue that needs to be solved. Be that problem-solver for them and they will pay you for it. You can use the idea to start your company and be on your way to being a great entrepreneur.

Don't be scared of jumping in. The water is warm and everyone is welcome in our pool.

CHAPTER 1: THE IDEA

"If you've got a great idea that would improve people's lives, just do it" – Sir Richard Branson

There is no harder step in this book than this - you need an idea! If you're reading this, you probably already have at least a slight notion of an idea in mind, but if not I can give you a little insight on where good ideas come from.

The first piece of advice is this: don't get held up on the idea. This means don't think of an idea and attempt to figure out all the small details right away. Those details will come over time. Take the idea and run with it.

WHERE DO IDEAS COME FROM?

1. YOUR WORLD
These are the spontaneous ideas that hit you in your everyday life. The appliance in your kitchen that desperately needs another function, the underutilized advertising opportunity in your morning commute, or the piece of software we know could optimize our workday. We tend to move through life quickly and accept things for what they are, but when you slow down and start to question the things around you, you'll find yourself inspired by life.

Many of these ideas you'll throw out—too expensive, not enough of a target audience—but once you start to see the world around you as open market for opportunity, you're bound to find a couple of ideas with real potential.

2. YOUR "BAD" IDEAS

Some of us are blessed with inspiration all the time. We come up with ideas constantly throughout the day, laughing many of them off as unrealistic, shirking others as poor concepts. James Altucher, famed writer of the Altucher Confidential[ii] says you should come up with ten ideas a day. You'll find that the more bad ideas you have, the more potential good ideas you'll have as well. Keep a note open on your mobile device or a notebook (later I will explain why you need a notebook on hand always) and write down every idea you have, no matter how foolish or grandiose it seems. When you go back from time to time to review the list, you may see the more realistic, accomplishable side of some of those ideas. Reading that list off to others can also be a launch point to discussion and the development of those concepts into something legitimate. The only way to guarantee an idea won't go anywhere is to ignore it.

3. YOUR WORKPLACE

We spend a lot of time criticizing our work environments. "I wish something existed to make this job easier" or "why don't they just make this thing already?" For example, a client of mine had an email server that went offline during Superstorm Sandy. While proper backup servers were set up, they too went down during the storm. The client had no email for a few days, and their business was significantly affected. This scenario was the inspiration for my app Email Phoenix, a backup mail service for the type of server that they use. Once the problem arose, the development of a cloud-based backup solution was relatively effortless. With so much technology at your fingertips, the workplace is a springboard for potential ideas. Start by identifying the weaknesses and you'll find yourself naturally developing solutions.

Allen Hancock, CEO of Watchman Monitoring had a similar story. As an Apple consultant in Baton Rouge, Louisiana he kept telling himself, "If only I knew the backups weren't working," when it came to a client who lost some files on their computer. Anyone who uses a computer knows how valuable your data is, and losing it can cause you to mentally lose it as well. He soon realized there was a better way, and decided to create an app for OS X users called Watchman Monitoring. The tool sends alerts to Allen when something is wrong with his clients' machines, including a failed backup.

4. COLLABORATIONS
Sometimes you have an idea that can't quite round out to completion, an idea that is half-baked, so to speak. Some of the world's best new inventions are not the efforts of one person, but a collaborative effort. Conversations with others in your field, even those you connect with on the Internet from the other side of the world, can lead to higher-level inspiration. Discussing your respective concepts with a colleague can lead to realization that while individually, you're only halfway there, but together, you've struck gold. Even casual conversations with friends of co-workers can lead to idea development. I can't tell you how many great concepts have been born on a cocktail napkin at a bar. Keep a non-disclosure agreement on hand for more serious collaborative meetings, but stay open to the idea of teamwork. Too many egos over the years have gotten in the way of what could have been great success stories.

5. FRIENDS AND FAMILY
You don't have to limit your collaboration to other business-minded folks either. Really listen to your friends and family. By paying attention to their daily complaints, you have the opportunity to find room for improvement in their lives as well as your own.

My mother is hard of hearing. I constantly receive requests from her to come up with something to improve the quality of her life. Sure, a lot of her complaints are just too large for me to resolve, but there have been several ideas that have launched some real concepts and developments that have been made to accommodate her disability. Think of your friends who are having trouble marketing their own businesses, or older family members who are struggling with modern technology. The people around you are an unending supply of problem-solving potential.

Just keep in mind that no matter what you come up with, your mother will probably think it's genius, so be sure to vet it out with someone less subjective.

6. DESIRE
Sometimes, you just have a desire. What is the one thing you wish you always could do? While my desire is to become Tony Stark (a.k.a. Iron Man), there are some who have more realistic dreams.

Take Riddhika Jesrani of Riddhikia Jesrani Jewelry. I met Riddhika while handling IT for a design firm in NYC. She was born in Bombay and brought up in the Middle East. At design school, she learned that she could create jewelry to express her creative outlet. This led her to designing her first pair of earrings. According to Riddhika, "This one pair of earrings was a hit. All my friends wanted the baubles I made, and I was more than happy to make them for them. One thing led to another, and the next thing I knew my best friend who worked on a big budget Bollywood movie called *Kabhi Alvida Na Kehna* showed my earrings to the designers on set. They liked them so much that I was contacted to make a bunch of pieces for the movie. "

Over the next five years, Riddhika worked on her jewelry. Her desire to make beautiful pieces fueled her to push further. She took a chance and did her first solo show in the Muscat, Sultanate of Oman. Her pieces sold quickly, and the show had a lot of press coverage.

That coverage, amongst other things, made her jewelry so popular, she decided to open her own studio in Bombay, and hire some employees. Over time, her pieces were getting more and more coverage, including a Cosmopolitan shoot for *Bridal Wear* magazine.

Riddhika credits the success the brand has gained to friends and family who believed in the product and who spread the 'bling love,' to insane amounts of luck. "I really think I have been in the right place in the right time, hard work and, of course, my crazy obsessive love for jewelry."

7. ASK AROUND
If you feel that you are bound for entrepreneurship, you can always ask potential clients for ideas. Much like finding weaknesses in your own company, you can call companies in the market you are interested in, and ask them what issues they need to deal with on a regular basis. Figure out what issues are happening at all of the companies. If they all share a common issue – there's your idea. Make that. After all, you know they will buy that product.

CHAPTER 2: WHAT TO DO WITH YOUR IDEA

1. WRITE IT DOWN!
In the immortal words of the *Van Wilder*[iii] movie: "Write that down!" On your phone, on your tablet, and/or in your notebook, jot down your overarching concepts, as well as the smaller ideas that go along with them.

What do you write down? Maybe a target audience, or a blogger you want to write to about your product. Any thoughts, ideas, impressions you have, get it down. Keep an 'Ideas' note on your phone to keep track of these notions. You'll find that once an idea hits, your thoughts will come in fast and furious. However, I assure you that the absolute worst feeling is coming up with something brilliant and then forgetting it a few hours later. There have been times when an idea has hit me in the shower. I will get out mid-shower, dry off my hands and write the idea down then finish the shower. As discussed earlier, keep track of your bad ideas as well; you never know when they may turn into ideas with potential.

2. SLEEP ON IT
When inspiration hits, you can become overwhelmed with the excitement and have the urge to jump into development right away. Give yourself a chance to let the idea percolate a bit. Some downtime will allow you to identify concepts that aren't legitimately achievable, and this time will also give you the

perspective to make good ideas even better. While I love to stay positive and encouraging, the truth is that most ideas we come up with do end up failing. A little sleep helps you remove the rose-colored glasses and see your ideas for what they really are. If in the morning the idea turn out to be shit, just take comfort in the fact that the more shit you throw against the wall, the more likely something will stick.

3. PLAY WITH IT

You've found divine inspiration, you've slept on it, and you still think it's solid. Now it's time to draw it out. Draw up an outline for how it will work, make a list of ideas for what it will be called, and sketch out ideas for a logo or branding aesthetic. Just get all the components down on paper in some fashion. When you move an idea from concept to visual you will find new components or directions that would not have presented themselves otherwise. By the same token, talk it out. Start discussions with others, even record yourself explaining your concept so you can find the weaknesses in your logic and hone in on the key fundamentals of what you're trying to achieve.

FIGURE IT OUT

Bruce Zutler, president of MCI Products Group and Inventors Association of Manhattan said it the best, "Not every idea is a good business." While this sentence can sound discouraging, it actually speaks to figuring out mistakes before they happen.

Bruce's company takes ideas and helps them become reality; whether it's prototyping and manufacturing, helping with patents, or even business coaching. He told me a story about a client of his who had a great idea for a product.

"My client was a podiatrist who had a great product idea. He had all the proper backup data, and had done all the research. This product was going to revolutionize a way in which he and other podiatrists did a particular type of procedure. When I asked, the client how prevalent the need was, he said that this procedure is performed approximately 100,000 times per year. I went on to ask, what would be the right price for a product like this? The second the client said only $5, I knew it was not going to be a good business."

"Let's break it down. If the product was brought to market and captured 100% market share the most the client would have made is $500,000; but that is assuming he is selling directly to his end customer. It is likely that some re-seller or distribution partner would be involved; thus the client's actual maximum sales would be only $250,000, once again, assuming 100% market penetration. Now subtract the cost of getting the product made, which is roughly 50%. Now the client is only making $125,000, at best. Most of the time a product like this might achieve a 10-20% penetration within the first 3 years, so a likely scenario would really earn the client only $12,500-$25,000 per year. Don't forget about marketing, tradeshows, investment in first production and inventory and a patent application; expenses that could easily approach $100,000. All of a sudden this "great idea" is a 4-5 year investment of time, money and energy before making a single dollar of profit, and not at significant levels." Worth it? Not on its own.

If the client has an established business, and this was a new product then maybe it would work, since much of the established marketing was already there which possibly could have increased market penetration to say 75%.

This is why I suggest you really think about what you want to build. Make sure there is a viable market that's large, and not limited in any way. When I came up with the idea for SignMyPad, I realized that signing a PDF document has such potential in so many markets. This realization allowed me to move forward and get it made.

CHAPTER 3: I'VE NAILED IT...NOW WHAT?

"Vision without execution is hallucination." – Thomas Edison

FOCUS

You must have focus when working on your project. I don't mean quit-your-job-and-do-nothing-but-work-on-this project kind of focus, but set aside time each day to work on it. I work on a few projects at once, but I focus on each one at a time to make sure it's on track. Even if you are focusing for ten minutes on the project, do nothing else but work on that project. This means no email, no Facebook, no TV, and no nothing.

TOOLS TO HELP YOU FOCUS

Here's where I repeat this piece of advice, to make sure it sticks, write down your ideas. I have multiple mobile devices, but I still prefer to write down my ideas in a notebook. For starters, I never need to worry if the notebook is low on battery power. Short of while I'm driving, I write down every idea I have. There have been times I've pulled over to write something down – safety first!

Aristotle Onassis, the shipping tycoon, gave this advice[iv]: "Always carry a notebook. When you have an idea, write it down. When you meet someone new, write down everything you know about them....THAT is a million dollar lesson they don't teach you in business school!"

Another great tool to help focus is a Kanban board. The Kanban board is a board that is broken into 3 columns:
> To Do
> In Progress (or Doing)
> Done

The methodology behind the Kanban board comes from the Kanban method created by David J. Anderson[v]. The method was originally designed for what's called "Just-in-time delivery" so products could be built and sent without overloading team members. Using a Kanban board allows you to figure out the steps from definition to delivery. I personally use my Kanban board to break up large projects into smaller tangible components. My board, which is made up of post-it notes that I can easily move items from one column to another, is on my wall right in front of me. I see it everyday when I go into my office. While my notebook is my daily to-dos for each project, the Kanban board shows me progress as a whole. For example if I wanted to update my website, I would have on my board the components:
> Update home page
> Increase Blog posting
> Adjust contact page

Then my to-do list would have the smallest pieces of the "Update home page" board topic, such as "move this line to another location," "change the font," "fix the grammar error here," etc. I can move the update home page post-in from To Do to In Progress when I'm starting the day, and then to the Done column once it's finished. There is an overwhelming sense of accomplishment when you can move an item from the To Do column to the Done column. Those little wins will help you move forward with your project and keep you motivated.

While I did say no email, no TV and no Facebook I did not say no Internet. Most of us need the Internet to build our projects. There are a lot of great online tools to help you focus. Tools like WorkFlowy[vi], Google Drive[vii], and Evernote[viii] are effective tools to keep you focused and productive. These tools allow you to have your data and notes anywhere you go, since they are in the cloud, but there is a big downside:

YOU HAVE TO REMEMBER TO CHECK IT!

Technology is great, don't get me wrong, but let me tell you a story. Back when I was in college I, as I am now, tried to be on the forefront of technology. I had a Palm Pilot where I would write down all of my assignments. I would put my Palm Pilot back in my bag and go about my day. But at the end of the day when I got back to my dorm, I would see friends, go to dinner, and forget to check my device. What good is writing it down if you aren't going to check it? Unless it's right in front of you all the time, you will forget to do things that need to get done. If you really want to use a cloud based product to maintain your to-do lists or Kanban board, I suggest using a tool that would display the website right on your desktop. For the Mac OS, you can use Web Desktop[ix] and for both Mac OS and Windows you can use an app called Snippage[x] which will take a snippet of a website and put it right on your desktop.

Another good way to gain focus is by exercising, whether it's ten minutes on a treadmill or ten minutes of yoga. Exercise helps you focus and being healthy allows you to keep your mind clear. I'm not saying you have to go out and get a trainer and drink only protein shakes, but going for a jog, doing some push-ups, or finishing ten jumping-jacks will help get your endorphins going and allow you to focus and be super productive.

Focusing on what you are working on is key when trying to get through those individual tasks on your to-do list. It's really easy in today's world to be distracted by emails, Facebook, or phone calls. Find a time and find a way to focus on your tasks so you can get through and get things done.

PROTECT YOURSELF

"What do you have when 100 lawyers are buried up to their necks in sand? Not enough sand!" That being said, the world is a messy place, and a lawyer can often make the difference between your idea's success and its failure.

Before you hire or talk to anyone about your amazing idea, you should get a NDA (non-disclosure agreement). As you move through the stages of idea development, speaking to others becomes more and more vital. Unfortunately, there are still people who act in their own self-interest, so you need to be smart. Have everyone you speak to about your idea sign an NDA stating that they will not steal your concept, or discuss it with anyone else who could potentially do the same. Even someone you trust could potentially mention your idea to the wrong person, however, by signing a NDA contract, it will make them far more aware of the importance of keeping quiet. Just like you would not have your dinner guests try their entrees before they're fully cooked, you don't want the public to learn about your idea before it's ready. If signing the NDA insults any of your friends/family/colleagues, just blame it on your lawyer.

Next, you are bound to receive some issues/threats from other companies whenever you introduce yourself as a competitor in the field. In the app world, it can be violations of end user license agreements. In other areas, it may be patent or copyright infringement. As you can imagine, everyone is out to protect himself, and the legal system often provides the means to do so. Before you panic and give up, review the threat with your own lawyer. Sometimes, it may be unjustified and easily squashed. In other instances, you may need to make minor adjustments to your game plan to avoid any legal controversy, and your lawyer can help you get there. I've had my share of legal attacks before, and so far none of them have done any permanent damage to my success.

PATENTS
For those who don't know, a patent is a legal document that shows you are the owner of an idea (or at best the first one to file a patent for the idea). This allows you the best opportunity to profit from the idea, since no one else can copy it. So should you get a patent?

It depends. The US Patent office received over 500,000 patent applications in 2012[xi]. The average length of time for a patent application to go all the way through to approval is 29.4 months[xii]. That's a long time to wait for your patent to be accepted. For those who are building software that's way too long to wait, since by the time your patent is approved the platform you are building on may be gone, but for those building a physical product you may have the time to wait. What's more, patents in the United States last twenty years so think about the lifetime of your product. Is your product going to last twenty years after the patent gets accepted? If so maybe you should think about getting a patent. If not, it may not be worth it.

There are very specific rules and instructions for filing a patent, especially regarding software. For example you cannot patent a mathematical equation and the Patent Office sometimes considers software a combination of mathematical equations – so how can one patent software? Let's look at the different types of patents and then we can figure out the answer.

TYPES OF PATENTS
There are three types of patents you can apply for according to the United States Patent Office:
    1. Utility Patent – "Granted to anyone who invents or discovers any new and useful process, machine, article of manufacture, or compositions of matters, or any new user improvement thereof" [xiii]

2. Design Patent – "Design patents may be granted to anyone who invents a new, original, and ornamental design for an article of manufacture"[xiv]
3. Plant Patent – "Plant patents may be granted to anyone who invents or discovers and asexually reproduces any distinct and new variety of plant"[xv]

For a physical product, you probably want to apply for a design patent since you are designing a new item that you plan on manufacturing. Unless of course what you are designing is a new tool to design other things. Then you would go for a utility or a design patent. For software, you would be clearly applying for either a utility or design patent based on the utility or design of the app itself, and not the code (which is just math equations).

A patent application is a waste if the patent already exists. There are many online tools to search if your patent exists already such as the US Patent Office Search[xvi] and Google's Patent Search engine[xvii]. If you are searching for a patent, I suggest searching for generic terms. For example, if you are looking into a software patent for the Apple app store, search for things related to 'mobile' as opposed to iPhone. There are patents that date back to the early 1980's that cover so much of the mobile space.

In discussions with my Intellectual Properties (IP) lawyer, I found out that to patent software you need to patent the components of your software that make it different than others. So our original patent was going to be for SignMyPad Pro and we were going to highlight the geo-tagging (adding the location and a time stamp to the properties) of the PDFs.

We applied for the patent on SignMyPad Pro, but after months of waiting we were rejected because there was a patent from 1994, that allowed for faxes to be displayed on a mobile device for signature, which is the core function of SignMyPad (and Pro).

Had I been more diligent in my own searches, I probably would have found the prior patent and not spent a few thousand dollars on a lawyer trying to patent SignMyPad, knowing it would be rejected.

Let's try to be positive. If you do your research and you find there isn't a patent for your idea, it's time to apply. You could try to apply yourself, but I highly suggest investing in an IP lawyer. IP lawyer prices range depending on state, their skill level, and, of course, the complexity of the patent. Their fees usually don't include any filing costs, so those need to be a part of your budget too.

Getting a patent is a lengthy, costly process, but in the end you will have rights to the only device that does what it does. No one else can copy your device for twenty years. The patent ensures your product a healthy long life, and saves you a lot of headaches during that lifespan.

CHAPTER 4: GETTING IT BUILT

"I built my talents on the shoulders of someone else's talent." – Michael Jordan

You've now come up with a great idea, really focused on it, and possibly protected your idea. Now, let's get it executed. You won't make any money if the product isn't real.

Not all of us can be Tony Stark, capable of building a generator in the depths of caves in Afghanistan. That's okay. There are places online where we can go for help. I'm a huge proponent of outsourcing what you can't do yourself. For Autriv, we outsource all of our programming because, despite my parents' pleas, I just don't know how to program.

You can outsource almost every part of your business (except the idea, of course). To really get a good understanding of outsourcing, I have outsourced the following section of "Why you should outsource" to president and owner of NeoSoft Technologies in India, Nishant Rathi.

If your tasks are best done outside, rather than inside, why choose outsourcing? You always have the power of choice. Apart from low costs, greater flexibility with time, and fulfilling the void for lack of expertise internally, it can give you space to ponder over greater pursuits, such as innovation. It enables you to give undivided focus to your core business process and implement the best practices. If you shy away from outsourcing, but your competitors don't, you are missing out on hidden potential and you may blunt your competitive edge.

Why Outsource Work?

- Are you utilizing your resources properly?
- Are your current practices supporting the latest technology?
- Are you working at optimum costs?
- Is there a faster and superior means to handle processes?
- Does your team have the knowledge and expertise to do the task assigned?

Think about it and make an informed decision. This should be your first step towards outsourcing and will get you started.

Companies with outsourced IT processes make a better transition towards new technologies with minimum disruption than the ones that are non-initiated to outsourcing. An outsourcing company will always have a backup plan in case of natural calamities, accidents, market fluctuations, or technical crises. Outsourcing will expose you to expertise offered at a global level.

If you select the right firm, a super league of technical experts can be hired on a part time/ hourly basis/ monthly basis or even fixed cost. They will make the maximum use of the latest technology and tools. Besides, that gets rid of the set up costs. You get a number of choices available and communication is relatively easy via chat/email/voice chat during project time.

One of the obvious reasons to outsource has been the lower labor cost. You get things done at relatively cheaper rates. Also, there might be a shortage of talent in a particular country, which spells the need for outsourcing. When companies need to build one-time applications that need high manpower resources and companies, outsourcing is often the best option to avoid expensive outlays for the short term.

HOW AND WHAT TO OUTSOURCE

So let's talk about what and how to outsource. There are multitudes of websites out there that offer outsourcing tools, but two of the major sites are Guru.com [xviii]and Alibaba[xix].

Guru.com is a site where you can hire anyone from programmers to designers to finance people. With Guru.com, you post your project, and allow for freelancers/outsourcers to bid on your project.

You can then ask bidders questions about specific skill sets. This is an important part of the vetting process. For the appropriate task, you can get portfolios and past work samples. Always check these to make sure the person is on the same page as you. When I first posted the project about SignMyPad on Guru.com, we asked the following questions (keep in mind this was 2010):

1. How many projects have you done in the past involving PDFs and iOS?

2. What version of the iOS SDK are you currently certified with?

3. How often will I get updates, and betas to work with?

What I was trying to get from applicants was to see how extensive their knowledge was with my project, and how close they could relate to the way I understood things. Remember, I don't know the first thing about programming, xCode (Apple's coding application), SDK's (software development kit), or PDF manipulation!

Once I had weeded out the bids that didn't satisfy my needs (either from their answers or their portfolio), I had them all sign the non-disclosure agreement.

Most of the companies bidding were in India, so enforcing a NDA was near impossible, but it helped my selection and set my mind at ease, since a few weren't willing to sign. The ones who didn't sign got cut. To the ones that were left, I sent them my idea. With my wife's help (see teamwork!), I was able to draw up a flow chart of images, which allowed the bidders to solidify their quotes. Then I picked the quote I thought was the best fit for my needs and SignMyPad was launched.

Alibaba.com is an international trading space where manufacturers put up their wholesale goods for purchase. When I decided that a stylus would be a good companion product to SignMyPad, I went to Alibaba.com. I ordered some samples from a few companies in China (yes, I had to pay for those samples). My interns at the time and I played with all the styluses I purchased and settled on two possible designs. We went back to the companies to find out if they could put magnets in the styluses. One company sent us a prototype right away, the other asked very important questions, such as where should we put the magnets, what size magnets, and which polarity should face outwards? Clearly we went with the second company. My interns did some research on where the magnets should go, and while it took two weeks longer to get a prototype than the first company, it was a much better product. Now, magnetic styluses are sold on the website and are a great supplement for users of SignMyPad.

Michael Friedland of Pawz Dog Boots used outsourcing to produce his dog booties. Late in 2005, Michael's father dog was having difficulties walking outside in bad weather. The chemicals used to melt snow and ice bothered the dog's paws. For a while his father, Gary, tied plastic bags around the dog's feet, and this is how he conceived his original idea for Pawz Dog Boots. Gary came up with putting a rubber balloon on the dog's feet. While a conventional balloon worked, Michael felt they could design something better. Michael and his team did the research, looked into companies around the globe who were producing products out of rubber and latex, found a company that had the desired skill set, and hired them.

Michael settled on a latex provider in Malaysia who made a great product and didn't break the bank. He was able to produce his idea and sell it online and to retailers. Pawz Dog Boots currently sells the product in 7000 locations in twenty-two countries. He has since brought production back to the U.S.

The people who you outsource to can be anywhere in the world. I've hired people in India, China, North Carolina, California, and Europe to do different parts of different projects. I've even moved the same project around to different people since each one had a slightly different skill set to get the job done.

Outsourced employees costs depend on location and skill set. From my own experience, outsourced employees in the United States costs anywhere from five times to twenty times that of India or China. But like the expression goes, "You get what you pay for." I have gotten faster turnarounds from my U.S. employees than my outside-of-the-U.S. teams. I'm not saying it's necessarily a bad thing, but it's just a fact. On SignMyPad for Windows, we actually spent more on a programmer in California for a weekend to install a component and fix a bug, than we did for the entire month with the team in India who built the whole thing.

An important consideration, with outsourcing, is communication. Not always is English the first language with outsourced companies, so sometimes instructions get lost in translation. When dealing with outsourced employees where English isn't their first language, it's best to make sure you both have a full understanding before any work is done. Whether that's using online translation programs, drawing pictures, or even hand signals in a video chat, make sure both sides 100% completely agree and understand the project, otherwise you'll be spending money on the wrong thing. The point of this book isn't to spend money, it's to make some.

WHAT NOT TO OUTSOURCE – IS THERE ANYTHING?

The answer is technically no but with one MAJOR exception. You cannot outsource the idea creation. The idea has to come from you: your idea, your vision, your dream. Everything after that can be outsourced. Here are a few examples of things you can outsource:

- Administrative Support – Companies like GetFriday[xx] and BrickWork[xxi] offer full-time virtual assistants who can handle all your administrative needs. From answering emails, to formatting documents, to ordering flowers for your spouse, there are people around the clock to help you. I have used GetFriday to do tasks for me, such as research a scanner for a client of mine. What took them three hours to do at $10 per hour allowed me to do something else for three hours. Had I done the work myself, I would have wasted $450 (my hourly rate is $150 for consulting), but instead I spent $30, and was able to help another client and get paid for my time. So for a net of $420, I didn't have to do six hours of work.

- Engineering and CAD design - When you are designing a product, you have to know your limits. When designing a physical product, you need a CAD (computer assisted drawings) design in order to build the product correctly. But maybe you don't know CAD. You can outsource this too. Draw a sketch of your idea to the best of your ability, and let your outsourced employees do the rest. When the iPad 1 was out, I had an idea for a business card scanner that would connect to the 30-pin connector. I don't know anything about electrical engineering, let alone CAD, to build this product. I found an engineer on Guru.com and explained my idea to him. I sent some crude drawings I had done, and whatever research I had gotten from Apple about their 30-pin connector. For a few bucks to get started, he started to build a prototype. The iPad was updated to have a camera, and so people made business card scanner apps via the camera but it was still a fun project to work on.

- Business Consulting – There are plenty of people available who want to help your business. They will help write business plans or help with financial documents.

- Sales and Telemarketing – Some of us are one-person shops and do not have the time to be on the phone all the time. While you should be selling your own product, if you could have two or three people making calls you can potentially sell that much more! You can hire sales people and telemarketers to get your product sold. Don't know how to write a telemarketing script? Outsource to the business consultants to get that done too.

- Graphic Design – This is a big one. Never forget that the product and company is your vison, but sometimes you need help with things like advertising design, marketing, posters, or maybe even business cards. Hiring a professional graphic designer will help get your message across beautifully. Find someone who understands your product so they can design components that conform to your ideals.

- Finance – Let's face it, not all of us are good at calculus. That's okay since you can outsource people to help with your finances. My biggest advice – don't hand off all of your finances to someone else. As the owner of the company, you need to know your numbers.

These are just some examples of things you can outsource. Start analyzing everything that needs to do be done for your idea to work – from initial concept through investing your profits once you've hit gold – and build the team you need to get there.

CHAPTER 5: TESTING

"Test fast, fail fast, adjust fast." - Tom Peters – author of Search of Excellence

Once your product has been made it's time for you to beta test. I use the term beta test loosely as many think beta testing is only for software, but you can beta test physical products as well.

Test, test, test, and then test some more. Do everything in your power to break your product. If you don't break it, a customer will. Find a way to use your product in every possible way every day. When I released SignMyPad, I used it with my day job as an Apple consultant. I had clients signing off repair work using the app and emailing them a copy of the document. When my wife and I were ready to buy our house. I told our realtor to only send me digital forms of our documents. While they were shocked, they luckily complied and I was able to sign all our documents with the app I had created. This was great because I was able to put the app (a new version) through its paces. Not only did I do my part to save paper, I found bugs with the app that I was able to fix before we released the new version to the public.

There's a funny photo out there on the internet with a caption that says, "I don't always test my code, but when I do it's in production." The phrase is saying that they don't test their software prior to it being released to public. Take it from someone who has been through the ringer with scathing online reviews after a buggy update. This is a BAD thing. Make sure you test your product in every way before releasing.

If you need help testing, you can find Quality Assurance (QA) testers. With software development, the company usually has a QA team you can hire, or you can outsource this to another company. QA testers will not only test your product they will find small issues that will help make the whole product better. Are things the right color? Are the warnings clear and concise?

Also, find beta testers. Beta testers are people you will give a pre-production unit to for free for testing. If this is an app, use tools like Test Flight[xxii], which will allow you to push new betas of your app to your selected team. For physical products find friends and family that you can give protoypes to for testing. Let them know, if they find an issue or it breaks you'll give them a new one hot off the press. Then reward them with the final product...and maybe a beer. For more expensive products, keep in mind that anyone you select to give a free beta version for testing, could eventually be a valuable client or at least a reputable testimonial.

If you are building software, another great piece of software to incorporate is Crashlytics[xxiii]. Crashlytics is a lightweight system you add to your app, and when your app crashes (and it will crash) in the real world you get email alerts with why. This software is free and it can really help make your software better.

CHAPTER 6: GET IT SOLD

"There is only one boss. The customer. And he can fire everybody in the company from the chairman on down, simply by spending his money somewhere else." – Sam Walton – entrepreneur, founder of Walmart and Sam's club

How much you should charge for your product is solely up to you. Maybe you are altrustic and this product can revolutionize the world, so you'll give it away for free. Maybe not. Physical products tend to have a one-time price associated with them. Once purchased that's all there is. Same with most software. Some of the best moneymaking products are software with monthly costs. Software like this is called SaaS (Software as a Service) It creates a great source of recurring revenue. Email Phoenix for example has a monthly fee associated with it. We established a lower price per month than if we just sold it outright, but we gain the monthly revenue which adds up over time.

Finding the right outlet for your product could be a hassle. Should you sell it online? Maybe look to get it into a big name distribution house like Walmart? Maybe there are already preestablished systems you can easily incorporate into (such as Apple's App Store, or Etsy.com). Of course there's always trying to get onto Shark Tank[xxiv].

One of the easiest ways to get to market is to go with an e-commerce site. You can build your own, or use existing systems (again the Apple App Store or Etsy.com). When figuring out how and which e-commerce site to use, just remember it needs to be clean and concise for users to purchase the product.

APP STORES

If you are building an app, the app store is the best way to get your software out there. **If you aren't building an app, just skip this section**. The App Store does a lot of the marketing for you (not all so don't rely 100% on it!). When I launched SignMyPad, once it hit the App Store people were already downloading it before I had even told anyone because Apple's App Store put it up in the New and Noteworthy section. I even got a phone call from a television studio who was interested in SignMyPad because their Apple rep saw it in the store!

There are many app stores out there, Apple, Google, Microsoft, Amazon, Barnes and Nobles, and then so many smaller systems. Let's talk about how to get into the big three.

APPLE

For the Apple App Store, either the mobile store on iTunes or the OS X app store via the App Store, you first need a developers account[xxv] with Apple. These accounts are $99 a year for each store (so $198 for both the iOS and OS X app stores). Not only do you get the opportunity to sell your product, you get access to Apple's beta software. With your account, Apple will provide you pieces of code called profiles that will associate your app with your account. Once you've built your app, you upload it to Apple's systems. Apple will then review your app. After that brief waiting period, if you are approved your app is live in the app store.

Apple charges you 30% of your desired price point for the app. For example, SignMyPad is listed at $3.99 in the App Store, of which I get $2.79 per purchase from Apple.

When you are uploading your app to Apple, there are details

that need to be figured out such as:

- The description of your app – Tell exactly what your app does. Do not just fill this area with marketing jargon.

- Keywords – When you search the App Stores, these are the words you think people will search for. As of this writing, you can not change your keywords once they are set, so think ahead for the future.

- Graphics – You need to upload screenshots of your app, so make sure they show your app in the best light.

- Price – Remember Apple will take 30% so choose your price point wisely.

- Legal – These are components such as Privacy Policy and Terms and Conditions. You should have these posted on your website.

Some things to note. During the review process, Apple tests to make sure your app doesn't crash, steal information, or create a problem. This doesn't mean the app might not crash on a users device, but that's why we installed Crashalytics. You want to make your app as stable as possible, but things happen. Apple will also deny your app if there are too many similar products in the app store. This means if you plan on making a fart app, think again.

Apple's payout schedule is 30+ days. This means for all the copies of your app you sold in August, you will be informed around September 15th and then paid for the first week in October.

GOOGLE

Google's app store (now called Google Play), is more lenient than the Apple App Store. When you upload your app, it's out there for sale. There is no vetting of your app for security or issues. Google believes you will test for that. Because of that lack of vetting, there are some nasty apps out there that can wreak havoc on users' devices. Don't let your app be that app. Google charges $25 for a registration fee to be a developer, as opposed to Apple's $99/year. The Play Store also does the same 70/30 split, but their payout schedule is much faster. At the time of writing this, Google just changed their payout schedule from the end of the month to the 15th of the following month. So for sales in October, you used to get paid the first week in November, now you get paid November 15th.

From my personal experience, programming for Google devices is harder than for iOS because I have found that the same Android OS works differently on different Android devices. I'm not saying this is a bad thing, but it is certainly a concern. SignMyPad works great on one device, but as soon as we change some code, it may cause an issue on another device.

One nice thing about the Google Play store is that you as the developer can respond to comments. The Apple and Microsoft stores do not have this - yet. So when someone leaves a comment, good or bad, you can reply to them, or say thank you.

MICROSOFT

Microsoft has recently started their own App store with the release of Windows 8, and their own tablet the Microsoft Surface. Microsoft charges $99/year to be a developer and at the time of this writing charges the same 70/30 split for the first $25,000 dollars, and then changes it to an 80/20 split.

OTHER STORES

There are other app stores out there, such as Amazon's Kindle store, Barnes and Noble's Nook store, Intel App Store, and Cisco's app store, to name a few. Most of these sell Android based apps, so if you are planning on releasing for the Google Play store, you might as well release it in these stores as well.

Stop skipping now, the rest is for everyone.

E-COMMERCE SITES

Maybe your product isn't an app. Maybe it's a piece of software, or a bag, or a component for your pickup truck. Building your own e-commerce site is the easiest way to do it. If you don't know how to build your own site, outsource it.

BEFORE WE BEGIN

There is one massively important component in the e-commerce world that you need to take into consideration: credit card payments. Everyone uses credit cards to purchase online, but you, as a reseller, need to make sure that data is transmitted safely and securely. Your own site security needs to be the number one concern before anything else. The worst thing that can happen is to have your site be hacked and credit card information be leaked. You will lose all the trust of your customers and their associates. There are many companies that already do credit card processing, such as PayPal and 2Checkout. Stick to using one of these companies to handle all your credit cards if you are going to build your own e-commerce site. This way you don't have to take on as much risk with users' personal information. Credit card processors usually charge a small percetage of the total sale, plus a few cents (so 2.9% of the total sale, plus 15¢).

PRE-MADE STORES

There are sites out there that will allow you to 'piggyback' on their technology of being an e-commerce site. 3dCart[xxvi] and Shopify[xxvii] are examples of this. Sites like these will handle everything for you. They have some basic layout choices you can pick from, but, more importantly, they will handle the credit card processing. These sites take a small percentage of your sale (not including tax and card processing fees), in exchange for you using their systems. If you have one simple product, this may be a good way to get started.

BUILDING YOUR OWN

Websites used to be difficult to build. You had to know all these codes to make things look the way they did. Not anymore. Now there are systems you can install on your server called a Conent Management System (CMS). Some of the more famous CMS's are Wordpress, Joomla!, and Drupal. Each have their own set of rules to follow, but the concept is the same. Whoever is hosting your website can install the base program for you, and you are up and running. And you can always outsource the programming to build your site.

I personally choose Wordpress because I have been using it since the beginning of my business and it has everything I need. If you look at any of my websites, you can see they all look different, but they are all based on the same system. The look was created by installing a theme. Someone built and coded a base look that I liked, and I was able to pay a few bucks to license the theme from them and install it onto my site. There are sites such as Theme Forest[xxviii] where you can purchase these themes. Giving your site the look you want is very important in selling your product. You want that product to 'pop' off the screen. Using a generic boring theme makes everyone think your product is boring too.

To give my site more features, I installed plug-ins. All three systems have the plug-in integration, but each have their own library of plug-ins. A plug-in is equivilent to a pre-made small program running on my website. These plug-ins are written by people all over the world, and submitted to the plug-in directory. Did I want to research all the coding to have my Twitter feed show on my website? No. So I found a plug-in to do that. There are plug-ins that can do anything, from security to e-commerce. Most plug-ins are free, but you can buy premium plug-ins[xxix] if you can't find a free one.

If you are going to build a Wordpress site here are a few plug-ins I always install and suggest you do also:

- Better WP Security – This plug-in allows you to review all the security options for your site. For example, by default all Wordpress sites have the same URL for administration access (www.yourdomain.com/wp-admin). Better WP security gives you options to change that.

- Viper's Video Tags – This plug-in allows me to use shortcode to easily put a video into my site. Say I wanted to put a video that's on vimeo onto my site, I could just do [vimeo]http://www.vimeo.com/movie[/vimeo] and the video is on my page. Image that instead of first figuring out the movie's proper URL and then figuring out the proper code to make it work.

- SNAP Autopublisher – This plug-in links to your social media accounts, so when you post a new post on your blog it will automatically blast it out for you to your Facebook and Twitter accounts.

- SEO Toast by Yoast – A helpful SEO plug-in that checks the viability of search engine optimization for your posts. It's very easy to use and to understand, and it makes your site easily searchable by Google and Bing.

To provide an e-commerce platform for a Wordpress site, I suggest using one of the following plug-ins:

- ECWID^{xxx} – With a free account you can start placing orders with ECWID. An easy shopping cart plug-in allows you to show off all your goods on your site. ECWID is just the shopping cart, you will still need to supply a credit card processor, such as 2Checkout. What I like about ECWID is how easily I was able to set up our first store. ECWID has paid plans that unlock other features, such as coupons but for most products you can get away with the free account.

- WooCommerce[xxxi] – This shopping cart experience is meant to allow you all the customizability you could ask for. WooCommerce on it's own is a simple shopping layout for your site. You still need a shopping cart, such as Mirijeh (the best one to use with WooCommerce) and a credit card processor. WooCommerce comes with its own set of plug-ins you can install. Want to have automatically have shipping labels calculated, use the UPS plug-in; want to have specialized coupons, use the WooCommerce coupon plug-in, and so on. WooCommerce allows for an immersive shopping experience and looks great on a page.

When having any site built on a CMS system, make sure you have a blog on your site. The reasons for this will be more detailed later in the marketing section, but having moving content on your site is great for site-link building in Google and allows your customers to realize you are knowledgeable, and still in business. Your blog posts do not always have to be 'selling' posts. Mix up your product posts with posts about things happening in the market or to you personally. Being honest on your blog is what really attracts customers. The idea is you want your customers to fall in love not only with your product, but also with your company.

Remember, a good product doesn't make a good company, your success is up to you.

CHAPTER 7: MARKETING

"ROI on social media is like hugging. You know it's there, but it is hard to measure." – Dave Murray – Social Media Manager

When it comes to marketing, watching Mad Men isn't going to teach you anything! Marketing since the advent of social media has taken on a new form. With social networking, you have to be immersed in this world and on top of your game. Social networking marketing is not an easy feat, but with a few small tricks, and some good knowledge you'll be on your way to being a marketing master.

The reason I write 'social networking' as opposed to 'social media' is because the number one rule regarding marketing on Facebook and Twitter is that you are networking. It's a two-way street. Much like meeting people in real life, you want to have conversations with members of your audience on these social sites.

If this were 'social media marketing,' it would be like you going to a conference, and me coming up to you to say "Hi, I'm Justin. Buy my product. Here's what it does," and then running away. Would you buy products from me? Probably not. But if I were to introduce myself, and talk to you about your needs, what solutions I may be able to provide for you, and show you how it will affect your business, then you would be interested.

Using tools like Facebook, Twitter, and your blog allows you to establish yourself as an expert in a specific field. Being an expert doesn't mean you've spent 10,000 hours studying the topic. It means you know something at minimum a little better than the other person in the conversation. With the Virtua Computers blog, I'm an expert in all things Apple. I use Twitter to answer people's Apple computer questions, and to ask my own. I have conversations with people not only to get answers, but also to establish myself as a person that knows this topic. Being an expert in the field you are working in establishes authority. Being an authority will make sales. People will purchase from someone who is the authority in their topic. With SignMyPad, Autriv is the authority in mobile PDFs. We make sure we post about how PDFs on your tablet will help your business and save the earth, and people recognize that.

BLOG
As I wrote earlier, you should have a blog on your site. When using CMS systems, each blog entry builds a new page on your site, despite it not looking like it. With this, search engines (Google and Bing in this case) will recognize that there are new pages and will index those pages. This helps when someone is searching for a particular term or phrase. Using SEO plug-ins will also help this. In Wordpress, SEO Toast by Yoast makes doing search engine optimization easy. I can put a specific word or phrase and make sure I'm getting the maximum viability for a search. This doesn't mean it will be the first thing found in a Google Search, but it helps. Let's do an example:

I'm writing a post about a feature in our new product, SignMyPad Cloud.

SignMyPad Cloud is an Active Document Management system for users of SignMyPad Pro. In this post I have discussed the feature regarding location services. In my SEO Toast area, I'll make the keyword 'location service.' SEO Toast will then score my post. Does it have the keyword enough times, but not too much? Do my graphics have the right comment and alt tag information. Is my readability of the post too complex? All of these components add up to give me a rating of my SEO. SEO Toast makes a nice clear way of understanding it with colored globes (red, orange, yellow, green). If my post is green, I'm good to go.

Google will then index the post and if someone does a search for "SignMyPad location" this post will find its way to the top.

Another element to getting to the top of Google with your blog is having other blogs link back to your post. These are called linkbacks. If people are writing about your product on their blogs, make sure they are linking back to your site or specific posts.

Users like to see how the company works, so keep that in mind on your blog. Take the time to post things such as the process of how your product is made, pictures of your office, or sharing others opinions of your product both the good and the bad. Allow them a taste of what your company is like. Share your culture with them.

SOCIAL NETWORKING SITES

"Twitter is the water cooler of the 21st century." Joel Comm, blogger, writer

FACEBOOK
Obviously one of the biggest contenders in the social networking world is Facebook. Now everywhere you look you see the famous blue F icon. I've even seen it on the bumper of a courtesy car. Facebook claims to have over one billion people on their site, and through their business site[xxxii], you can target the right audience.

Let's say you were making a widget, and you took out a traditional ad in a magazine or newspaper. You have to assume that at least 50% of the readers of said magazine or newspaper aren't even widget users. You've now wasted a lot of money and potential sales. With Facebook ads, through their business site, you can target widget 'likes' and reach a much bigger audience. To do this, you first have to create your Facebook Business page. On there you will promote your product, interact with customers, and post updates. You can do a lot of updating and promotion from your blog with a plug-in (like the SNAP plug-in). You want people to see these updates so they can share or like it. This is great feedback from your customers. Once your page is built, you can now take out a Facebook Ad. You target your widgets to your specified target, such as males or females, their age, or location.

Here is an example. Let's say I wanted to promote my app, NYCTruckFood. NYCTruckFood is an app that lets users know where their favorite food trucks are in Manhattan. Thanks to everyone's personal data entered into Facebook I can target people who only live in NYC or the outer boroughs. Does this mean I don't want people in California knowing about NYCTruckFood? Sure I do, but if they are going to vacation in NYC, there are other ways to get to them. Since I want to keep my costs down on the Facebook ad, I want to directly target people in the NYC location. So starting a new ad on Facebook, the site tells me my audience is 176,000,000 people. This is the entire Facebook network around the world. As soon as I choose that I want to target New York, NY and cities within ten miles, the target drops to 3,800,000 people. For NYCTruckFood we want a really broad audience, so maybe we'd leave it like this, but we should try to target better. The ad defaults to users ages thirteen and up. When was the last time you saw a thirteen-year-old walking around Manhattan during lunch time ordering food from one of the famous trucks all by themselves? So we change the ad to twenty-two years old and higher (allowing for people in the workforce). We've now dropped 600,000 people to achieve a target of 3.2 million people. This works for us.

For testing purposes, I added the 'Food and Dining' interest into my target, which dropped my audience down to 1.1 million people. I've now gone from 176 million to 1 million, and I know I have a very high chance of getting those 1 million interested because they fit who my target is.

I have my product page, where I can interact and engage with my audience and I have my ad that will direct them to my site and hopefully convince them to download the app. (Note: you can advertise the hell out of anything you want, but it won't guarantee 100% that someone will download your product – especially if it's garbage.)

TWITTER

Twitter has exploded in the last few years. It was originally built as a small form way to communicate with your friends. Its 140-character limit was designed since you used to have to text your tweets. Back when it first came out a lot of tweets were, "I'm eating soup for lunch." But now it's a great place for brands to push their products, get the word out and really interact with their audience.

Like all social media and marketing, Twitter has its own pros and cons.

PROS
1. It's quick – Have something to say, imply, or question? Form a quick 140-character tweet and click send.
2. It's easy to read – The 140-character limit means companies can't subject you to the standard marketing mojo they are used to spilling. They have to compress their message to something that will truly catch your eye.
3. It's very easy to link to other Twitter accounts and topics. If you are on Twitter you already know (and if you aren't here is your base lesson) that @someone will link to that person. It makes it very easy for them to respond. Note: starting a tweet with @someone allows that person to see it as well as any mutual followers. Using @someone

in the middle of your tweet means everyone who follows you can see it. Here's an example:

  a. "@justinesgar I love your book dude!" Only I and anyone who follows both of us see that, unless someone looks at your full timeline.
  b. "I'm reading the @justinesgar book. It's awesome." Now everyone who follows you will see that and I will get a notification.

On Twitter, the hashtag (#) is used to specify a topic or keyword. This makes promotions very easy. If you check out the Autriv Twitter account (@Autriv) you will see we always hashtag our products such as #SignMyPad or #HomeBase. This creates a clickable topic users can see others posting about. On the NYCTruckfood.com Twitter account (@truckfoodnyc – yes I know it's a bit confusing), you can see I use the hashtag "yum" or "nyc." Using the hashtag allows you to find things in Twitter's search engine.

CONS

1. It's quick – Twitter moves very fast, and depending on how many people you follow you may miss an important tweet. While you can always scroll back to see older tweets, you'll get inundated with the stuff you've missed while scrolling.
2. There is a lot of crap on it. While there are plenty of legitimate things on Twitter, much like the rest of the Internet, there's plenty of crap on it. Not to say following a porn star is crap, but unless they are promoting something you want, there isn't much they will say that will affect your daily life. Try to limit who you follow to people of like interests.
3. Everyone has an opinion. It's easy to get very different answers to the same question on Twitter. Be open to the different answers, but think wisely as to which is the right one to listen to when it comes to your larger goals.

TWITTER SEARCH

The Twitter search engine[xxxiii] is a great tool to find people who talk about topics you like or want to respond to. For my Apple consulting company, I routinely search Twitter for hashtags like #machelp, #OSXuhoh, or #SOSapple to find people who have questions. I can jump in and try to help them. Note, I didn't say sell them on consulting, I said help them. These people need help, so help them. If they like you, they will buy your product. Worst case is you help them for free and their computer is working better which makes them happy. Best case is they will sign up for my services and suggest all their friends do too.

INSTAGRAM

If a picture tells 1000 words, Instagram can tell over a billion words. Instagram is a great place to post photos of your work or products being used. Use Instagram to tell a story about your product. Do a 'behind the scenes' on how your product is made using Instagram photos. That would be cool to see ☺.

VINE

Vine is a relatively new player to the game. Vine allows you to create 6-second movies to share. The movies are quick, so get your story in there fast. I thought about doing a Vine Q&A for #MacHelp. But I haven't quite gotten it ready yet.

MYSPACE

Amazingly to some people, MySpace is still around. As of June 2012, MySpace had 25 million unique visitors[xxxiv] in the United States alone. So why is MySpace still kicking? Because of the music industry. If you do anything involving music, you should be on MySpace. Forgetting some recent troubles MySpace has gotten into (re: June 2013, MySpace deleted their "classic MySpace" user accounts causing public outcry and lawsuits), MySpace is still the platform for people to release new music. If Justin Timberlake owning it isn't a sign of its potential, what is?

BLOGGERS

Love 'em, hate 'em, need 'em. You need other people to write about your products. Never forget the old adage: "All press is good press." Many people try to put a kibosh on bad press, but sometimes you can't. It's also not necessarily about what the article says, but how you respond to it.

When I launched SignMyPad, there was a request from someone to make a special version that had some new features. To make it easy for the client to download, I just posted it to the Apple App store for $99. Once they downloaded the updated version, now called SignMyPad Pro, I just left it on the store. No harm, no foul. When our interns started to reach out to bloggers to promote SignMyPad, we gave away free copies of SignMyPad Pro. One blogger for Wired decided to do a review.

Now the story I'm about to share is clearly all from my point of view, but here's how the day SignMyPad was on Wired went.

On a Wednesday in the summer of 2011, roughly around 8:45 a.m., I go into my office to check my daily websites. I see an article on Wired Gadget Lab about SignMyPad Pro. I got super excited. I believe I said something to the effect of "OMG we are on Wired's website!" I then read the article.

The writer wrote about how expensive the app was. It was obvious from the review that he didn't even try the app out, but decided to quote part of someone's iTunes review. He continued to rip us for asking for users' email addresses so we can say thank you for purchasing our app. (Apple doesn't give developers your personal information, so we had no other way to say thanks other than by asking, and it wasn't mandatory to tell us). The author thought we were collecting emails so we can spam them.

By 9:00 a.m., I was furious. I had some other work to do that day, but couldn't concentrate on any of it because of this article. I turned to my Facebook friends for advice. I got a lot of "Sue him for libel" remarks, which while heated sounded like a great idea, I knew it wouldn't have solved anything.

By lunchtime, we decided to comment on the original article. We posted that we would have a video on our site explaining our reasons for the high priced app and what we were going to do to appease customers, and especially the author of the original article. In our video, and on the post, we said that we would lower the price of the $99 version to $10 and keep it at $10 for each good comment about our app in response to the article. So for each post, the $10 price stood for another day. Not only did we get a handful of positive comments, which kept the $10 pricing for 8 days (before going to it's new normal price of $19.99), the whole ordeal made us more than one month's income in two days! Even though the article didn't put SignMyPad or SignMyPad Pro in the best light, we were still able to sell a lot more copies, and it got the name out there.

"Any press is good press." We took a bad review and turned it into a positive return.

When you have a product, get it out into people's hands so they can write about it. Send them free copies or samples. The more people write about it on the Internet, the easier it will be found which results in more sales.

Starting a cake ball bakery? Send free samples to food writers and restaurants. You'll become the new 'in' dessert. Make a magnetic stylus and send a bunch to bloggers with a free copy of an app to show off how the stylus works.

Find ways to get your product in front of these bloggers, and whether they love it or not, let them voice their opinion.

Maybe they'll spark a thought on how to make your product even better.

HARO

Another great online resource is Help A Reporter Out (aka HARO). HARO is an email that you'll get three times of day with requests for people to share their experience to a writer who is doing an article. Answering writers' inquiries is a great way to prove your expertise in the field. Get quoted as the CEO or inventor gets your name out there. The HARO email is broken down into sections such as Business, Green, Fashion, High Tech, etc. Thanks to HARO, I've been quoted in many magazines and even *The Wall Street Journal*. Depending on the inquiry I will respond as the CEO of Autriv Software Development, maker of SignMyPad or CEO of Virtua Computers, a NYC-based Apple consulting firm. I do this not to be pretentious, but so that my name, my company and possibly my product get listed. When you read an article in *The Wall Street Journal* you know the people who are being quoted are knowledgeable, if not the expert, in their field. You can be that person too.

ADVERTISING

Traditional advertising is far from dead, even when it comes to apps. A good ad placement could make your product shine. While traditional advertising in magazines and newspapers is usually expensive[xxxv], you can advertise on websites for a far better price.

Figure out your target market and advertise on sites that reach that market. The Watchman Monitoring product, for example, is meant for Apple consultants and advertises on tech sites frequently visited by Apple consultants. Advertising in magazines that Apple consultants read has opened doors to larger opportunities. For Allen, the CEO of Watchman Monitoring, the process of advertising has led to interactions with the site owners, getting interviewed, and write-ups over and above the traditional ads. This allows people to have a better understanding of the product and has resulted in a higher purchase rate.

WORD OF MOUTH

Word of mouth advertising is great, when people are saying nice things about your product. At the same time, an upset customer will make sure their point is heard (especially with how easy it is today thanks to social platforms). You can't control how word of mouth advertising works, so you have to do your best to make sure you are always getting the best words spoken about your product – meaning have a great product. Make sure your product packs a punch with a particular group of people. SignMyPad, for example, is a great tool for lawyers since it doesn't require documents to be on a central server, nor require an Internet connection to just sign a document. Thanks to these security features, SignMyPad has been talked about a lot at law conferences. I was never at (or invited to) any of those conferences, but all of a sudden I saw more tweets about our product and a spike in sales.

For Pawz Dog Boots, Michael's father had a set of boots on his dog, and people would stop him when he was out walking his dog. This allowed other dog owners who loved them once they saw them to find out about the boots. This guerilla marketing tactic turned into positive word of mouth marketing, causing a high increase in sales.

CHAPTER 8: INTERNS AND FRESH GRADUATES

Let's be honest, the economy, while on the upturn, isn't that great right now. Everyone is looking for a job, and if you are in college or just graduating, it may take some time before someone hires you. Everyone wants someone with experience, but if a person can't get a job, how do they get experience?

You as the new entrepreneur should be looking to hire these interns and fresh graduates. It just makes a lot of sense. For starters, interns and fresh graduates can be free, or minimal cost (buy them lunch, give them college credit, or a small per diem – just don't treat them like slaves to your business). Use interns and graduates to handle things like blog postings, or sending emails to prospective reviewers. Give them the routine tasks that **need** to get done, as well as challenging tasks to help them learn about your business.

I once gave an intern a challenge in which he had to get a certain number of reviews online for SignMyPad. If he hit the number, he would get a cash prize. Also on that challenge was to figure out how we could make the magnetic stylus that we sell. He was motivated to learn, as well as win his prize. He worked hard, and got the reviews that we wanted to see online. He also found websites that showed X-rays of the Apple Smart Cover, which allowed us to see the magnetic placement. Using Alibaba.com to get some samples, we were able to produce the product we wanted to make and now the magnetic stylus is for sale.

Interns and fresh graduates are great for handling the smaller tasks, even some that you may outsource to a virtual assistant. They are usually in your office, so you can get real-time results. If there are questions about the tasks you can ask or answer right there, instead of waiting for responses from overseas partners.

In addition, these employees are always willing to learn. They are like sponges for the knowledge you can share with them. Make sure you constantly teach them something new, so they don't become drones. Teach them the tricks you are using to become successful. Hey, maybe even buy them this book.

CORPORATE CULTURE

Long gone are the days of job security out of college. Long gone are the 9 to 5 days with an hour lunch break. Long gone is the sit at your desk, do your TPS reports, and punch out philosophy. Now companies are looking to build culture. Look at companies like Zappos and Google for how their corporate culture affects their employees. No more drones, now you have employeneurs (employee + entrepreneurs). People who want to work, learn and create while on the job.

When starting off, it's very important to ground the roots of your culture. Start with a mission statement and feed from there. For Autriv, and especially SignMyPad, our culture is built around saving people money while being environmentally conscious. Our goal is to have a low carbon footprint, while creating great software that helps people. Note, our culture is not to make money (which would be great), or to be the best software company in the world (which would also be great). Our culture is about something greater by helping our users. SignMyPad allows you, the user, to save money and time (which in turn saves more money), which is the way we want it to be.

Corporate culture isn't only about Hawaiian shirt Fridays, it's about legacy. What is your legacy going to be?

CHAPTER 9: YOU ARE SELLING – NOW WHAT?

Congratulations on getting this far. It's been a hard, long journey but you are selling a product that you came up with. How awesome is that?

So now what?

Start with thank you. While this should be common knowledge, sometimes we need to be reminded to say thank you to our customers. A personalized thank you is much better than the automated email with their invoice. Everyone who purchased your product is a human being, so why not treat them like one?

We've just implemented a new policy that when someone buys our stylus, we write a little thank you note on the invoice that ships with the product. For apps, it's harder since none of the app stores let you know who is purchasing your product, but the Google Play store does allow you to respond to comments. Make sure you take advantage of every opportunity to say thank you, even if you users think you are just harvesting their emails.

GET FEEDBACK

Get feedback from everyone (yes, including your mother if possible) on your product. Everyone's going to have an opinion so listen to all of them, but don't act on all of them. We've had many suggestions from our amazing user base, but some were

so outlandish we just had to decide against it. We're sorry for that, but thanks for downloading. When someone gives you feedback, thank them for their help and opinions. Even if the feedback is so far out there, the user still took the time from their day to think about your product and send you a note.

SUPPORT YOUR PRODUCT

"You want to be extra rigorous about making the best possible thing you can, find everything that's wrong with it and fix it. Seek negative feedback, particularly from friends and family." Elon Musk - entrepreneur, founder of PayPal, CEO of Tesla, and Space-X

It's inevitable that some people will have issues with your product. Maybe they used it in a way you didn't expect, maybe they couldn't assemble it properly, who knows but it's bound to happen. These people need your help. Some users will do whatever it takes to get in touch with you. My father told me that users sometimes call my parent's home to find me just to ask me a question. People are dedicated when something doesn't work right.

Think about how hard it was to build that latest Ikea flürgenstein (this is a made up product for those playing the home game). Ikea provides services to come to your home and build the stuff for you![xxxvi] How is that for great support? Need help? No problem, we'll come to you and help you. Be the Ikea for your product. You may not necessarily need to go to your client's home to help them, but make sure you give your clients plenty of ways to get in touch with you for help. For SignMyPad, we have multiple ways of getting in touch with us, via Twitter, our support site, and via email. Our address is available also for anyone who wants to send us snail mail. On Email Phoenix we even have an online chat feature to interact with users having issues.

If you are just starting out, make sure at minimum you have a support email that you can share with everyone. Make it easy – support@your company.com, or help@domain.com. No matter what happens, always help your customers. If they scream, type in all caps, or call you names (yes all three have happened to us), just remember they are the paying customers who spent their hard earned money to buy *your* product and are allowing you to live the dream.

Here's an example of an email our support team would get:

I just downloaded your app and it won't open my document! This sucks, your company sucks, and I can't believe Apple would let your sucky app be the app store! Sincerely, Pissed off

Here is our response:

Dear John - We are sorry about the technical difficulties you are incurring with our app. We would love to help you. Without seeing the document you are trying to open, we can only guess that the file is not a PDF. SignMyPad will only open PDF type files. If this is not the case, please let us know what type of document you are trying to open, and if possible send us the document so we can test it for you. We assure you we can help you get this issue resolved quickly. Thank you and thanks for downloading SignMyPad. Sincerely, The Autriv team.

See what was done there? We kept calm, provided a clean concise answer, didn't place blame, and already set it up for a follow up. We offer our help, explain what we think the issue might be and give the user some steps of what to do next. We also thank them for downloading the app, because even if they are upset, we want to thank them. Two possible outcomes come from our response:

1. The user never responds. Either they figured it out, or they didn't – we'll never know. Even if we send

another follow-up email. This usually happens when the person is **so** upset by the issue they just get rid of the product

2. They do respond. Either they say 'thank you' and figured out the issue, or they attach the document in question and we keep helping them until the issue is resolved and they are happy.

In our case SignMyPad is only $3.99, of which we make $2.79 (70%), but we certainly do not use that price point as a determination of how much we help our users. We know that we want all our users to be happy no matter what, which leads to great word-of-mouth marketing.

If you think I'm being too preachy about how we do things at Autriv, let's take another example of supporting your product.

Zappos, the Internet shoe store is a great example regarding customer service. Not only does Zappos offer a 100% guarantee of their product by providing returning shipping labels, but they make all of their employees spend some time doing customer service. This allows all the employees to be knowledgeable about what their customers' needs are. Also, there are stories that you can call Zappos customer service and complain about any product, even something they don't sell, and they will try to help you.

Another example, albeit another shoe company is a company called Shoes of Prey[xxxvii]. Shoes of Prey allow women to completely customize their shoe from the heel, to the toe, fabric, and more. Each shoe is individually hand made and shipped to you. You can now own your very own one of a kind shoe. What's great about Shoes of Prey is their service. Not only do you get your shoes in a dust bag, but you get a thank you card, but you can get a full refund if you aren't happy. A full refund on a completely customized solution? That's amazing service.

All companies will provide some level of service, but if you want clients to love your product you need to provide the best customer service.

MAKE UPDATES
If your product is a non-tangible item (such as an app), updates are easy. Your product updates follow the same steps you took to get your application made the first time. Make sure any update you release is a true update. Fix bugs (thanks to feedback and your support issues), add new features and maybe a fresh coat of paint.

For tangible items, it could be tougher. Yes you could release a new version with a sticker on the box saying 'New and Improved,' but realize that the owners of the original version probably won't buy the new version. (Unless of course you are making iPhones, then everyone wants the new one.) When selling a new updated version, make sure you adjust your marketing to target new customers.

TAKE OWNERSHIP
I don't mean of your company, I mean take ownership of the problem. This goes for your employees too. Everyone should take ownership of an issue or problem that comes their way, and do whatever it takes to get it fixed.

When you are looking to hire people, make sure they are in the like mind of taking ownership. When I started working in the IT field, my soon to be employer asked me a question that would test my ownership of the problem.

The question was: "A client calls, and says the CEO of the company is leaving for a conference in a few hours and his sixty page presentation isn't printing, and he needs it for the conference. What do you do?"

Many people, especially in the IT world, would answer with very technical answers, such as check the USB cable, are you printing to the right printer, etc. Doing this passes the ownership back to the CEO. It must be his fault something is wrong, right?

Taking ownership in this example would be going above and beyond. An answer like, "Send me the presentation and I'll print it for you right now and bring it to you (or FedEx it to your conference) and then fix your printer while you are away," clearly shows ownership of the issue. You are not only helping your client, you are making them love you even more. Love for you, or your product, means more sales.

HIRE EMPLOYEES
Congratulations, your product is bringing in a lot of money and you are now able to hire people for your company. Let's discuss.

Steve Jobs (yes *that* Steve Jobs) often said "Make sure you are hiring only A-players. Hiring B-players will only hire other B- or even C-players." Don't fear hiring someone who is smarter, better, faster, or more good looking that you to get the job done. Hire the person who is qualified, even if they are better than you.

Jobs continued discussing how hard it was to find A-players and that you could look internally for them. Unfortunately if you are a one-person company, how can you hire from the inside? Well, do you still have your intern or graduate employee who has now been inundated with your corporate culture? Look no further. Give them a job because you know you can trust them and they have proven themselves to you.

KEEP TRACK OF SALES
You need to keep track of your sales. You want to know where your money is coming in from right?

There are many schools of thought on this. You could use something as simple as a spreadsheet document, or complex like a custom database.

If you decided to go the database route, I suggest tools like Filemaker, since it's cross-platform and could be server based or some online options such as Zoho Creator and Track Via.

If you are doing an app, there are some great tools you can use. For example, if you are selling in the Apple App Store you should have AppViz. AppViz is a paid application that will download data from Apples site and give you a clean way of reading how much you made each day, the reviews from around the country and your rankings.

Figure out what method works best for you, and stick with it.

CHAPTER 10: KNOW WHEN TO LET GO

"Failure doesn't mean you are a failure it just means you haven't succeeded yet." - Robert H. Schuller – Famed Televangelist and motivational speaker

In early 2010, a software company that was adored by the Apple community was going out of business. There were many clients still using their software, and with them closing their doors all those clients would be without support or updates. This was an opportunity for us to build a new piece of software. One that would do all the things the original software did, and much more. As an Apple consultant, I took a two-way approach, figuring out what the client wanted and what the consultants wanted. It all sounded well and good, until disaster struck.

The software we were building, called BlackBook, was going to be the ultimate in contact software. It would allow users in an organization to share an address book, much like the original software did. It also allowed for the administrators to easily recover deleted contacts that happened oh so often with the original software. One thing we really wanted to add was a way to get these contacts on users' mobile devices. Of the whole project's ten months of development, eight months were dedicated to this one component. We fell into what we refer to as 'feature creature.' By the time we finished BlackBook, we were too late to the market. Many users had switched to other platforms and after a year of little sales we pulled BlackBook from the market.

There are two lessons here. The first is to release a minimum viable product (MVP). Get version one out the door. You can always add onto it later.

The second lesson is to be okay with terminating sales. You have to learn to say, "It's okay we failed." Don't think that if you keep adding features the product will miraculously pick up in sales. Instead of wasting more time and money on a failed project, pick up the pieces and start again.

CONCLUSION - FINAL STATEMENTS

I hope this book has helped simplify what is a complex thing of starting your own business and getting your product "appitalized." You will receive push back from everyone, including those who you thought had your back. You can and will persevere.

Starting a business isn't about the money, even though it helps. It's about living for your passion. It's about making a difference in the world. It's about making your dreams into a reality.

There will be good days and bad days. There will be times of money and times of none, but just keep going.

Don't stop!
Make it bigger!
Make it better!

You will soon realize you are living a life doing what you love to do. Wouldn't that be wonderful?

RESOURCES

i http://www.nydailynews.com/entertainment/tv-movies/americans-spend-34-hours-week-watching-tv-nielsen-numbers-article-1.1162285

ii http://www.jamesaltucher.com

iii http://www.imdb.com/title/tt0283111/

iv http://www.forbes.com/sites/drewhansen/2011/08/15/why-richard-branson-and-i-always-carry-a-notepad/

v http://en.wikipedia.org/wiki/Kanban_board

vi www.workflowy.com

vii http://www.google.com/drive

viii http://www.evernote.com

ix http://code.google.com/p/webdesktop-macosx/

x http://snippage.gabocorp.com

xi http://www.uspto.gov/web/offices/ac/ido/oeip/taf/us_stat.htm

xii http://www.uspto.gov/dashboards/patents/main.dashxml

xiii http://www.uspto.gov/web/patents/howtopat.htm

xiv http://www.uspto.gov/web/patents/howtopat.htm

xv http://www.uspto.gov/web/patents/howtopat.htm

xvi http://www.uspto.gov/patents/process/search/

xvii http://www.google.com/?tbm=pts

xviii http://www.guru.com

xix http://www.alibaba.com

xx http://www.getfriday.com

xxi http://www.brickwork.com

xxii http://www.testflight.com

xxiii http://www.crashlytics.com

xxiv http://ww2.abc.go.com/shows/shark-tank/casting?nord=1

xxv http://developer.apple.com

xxvi http://www.3dcart.com

[xxvii] http://www.shopify.com
[xxviii] http://www.themeforest.net
[xxix] http://www.codecanyon.net
[xxx] http://www.ecwid.com
[xxxi] http://www.woocommerce.com
[xxxii] http://www.facebook.com/business
[xxxiii] http://search.Twitter.com
[xxxiv] http://en.wikipedia.org/wiki/Myspace
[xxxv] From my personal experience
[xxxvi]
http://www.ikea.com/ms/en_US/customer_service/ikea_services/
ikea_services.html#assembly
[xxxvii] http://www.shoesofprey.com

Made in the USA
San Bernardino, CA
04 March 2016